Imagine the ultima
and asks you so

C000252740

When God asks...

10/10

By Richard Wilkins

First Print 2000
Published by cantecia
PO Box 454   Northampton   NN4 0GJ

cantecia is an imprint of Ten out of Ten

ISBN 0 952819864

Cover design by Richard Wilkins
Printed by Candor Print, Northampton

DEDICATION

To the child who lives within us all

FOREWORD

Please resist the temptation
to simply skip through these pages.
Instead, stop a while,
and follow the wisdom of your own answers.

INTRODUCTION

This book changed my life. It can change yours. It changed my life, not because I wrote it, but because I read it. I found that although my head was reading the questions, my heart was answering.

This book showed me how most of the time we are not living the life we really mean to live, or being the person we really mean to be. Simply because we have forgotten, and allowed our heads to deprive our hearts.

This book is to show you where you could improve your life, *not* to show where you are going wrong, the two are very different.

This book is a reminder of the life you could be living, giving you the opportunity to be the person you really mean to be, *ask your heart*.

Imagine God, the ultimate guest comes to dinner and begins asking you some simple questions about your life....

When God asks....

*How do you see your future
if you don't change?*

What will you say?

When God asks....

*Do you complain
about the lack of flowers
or do you plant seeds?*

What will you say?

When God asks....

*Do you create happiness
or do you chase after it?*

What will you say?

When God asks....

*Do you try to understand
as much as you want
to be understood?*

What will you say?

When God asks....

Do you see through my many disguises?

What will you say?

When God asks....

How many people do you love?

What will you say?

When God asks....

*Do you encourage
more than you criticise?*

What will you say?

When God asks....

*Do you place as much importance on how
you think as how you look?*

What will you say?

When God asks....

*Do you give as much energy to your dreams
as you do your fears?*

What will you say?

When God asks....

Do you listen as much as you talk?

What will you say?

When God asks…

Do you talk to strangers
before they talk to you?

What will you say?

When God asks....

*Do you see the good in people
as clearly as you see their faults?*

What will you say?

When God asks....

Do you make friends easily?

What will you say?

When God asks....

*Do you notice
when your prayers are answered?*

What will you say?

When God asks....

*How often are you the first
to say sorry?*

What will you say?

When God asks....

*Do you learn by other's mistakes
or do you insist on struggling
with your own?*

What will you say?

When God asks....

*How easy is it for you to share
in the success of others?*

What will you say?

When God asks....

*Does your honesty consider
the feelings of others?*

What will you say?

When God asks....

*Have you discovered the difference
between wanting and needing?*

What will you say?

When God asks....

*Have you already achieved goals
you thought would make you happy,
but didn't?*

What will you say?

When God asks....

Do you leave much unsaid?

What will you say?

When God asks....

*Are you aware that every reaction
to every situation
is a choice?*

What will you say?

When God asks....

How does your pride help you?

What will you say?

When God asks....

How important is it for you to own?

What will you say?

When God asks....

*Do you learn most
from good times or tough times?*

What will you say?

When God asks....

*Do you appreciate as much
as you take for granted?*

What will you say?

When God asks....

Do you smile at people
before they smile at you?

What will you say?

When God asks....

*Do you spend much time exploring
your potential?*

What will you say?

When God asks....

*How much care do you give to what
you put into your body?*

What will you say?

When God asks....

Do you celebrate the small things?

What will you say?

When God asks....

Do you search for wisdom?

What will you say?

When God asks....

How often do you hold on
when you could let go?

What will you say?

When God asks....

Do you review your opinions?

What will you say?

When God asks....

*How much time
do you dedicate to children?*

What will you say?

When God asks....

What will you be remembered for?

What will you say?

When God asks....

*Do you want other's
dreams to come true?*

What will you say?

When God asks....

*Do you free yourself
by forgiving others?*

What will you say?

When God asks....

*What changes would you make
if you had your life again?*

What will you say?

When God asks....

Do you take your life too seriously?

What will you say?

When God asks....

*Do you struggle before
you ask for help?*

What will you say?

When God asks....

*Do you walk far in the shoes of others
or do you just try them on?*

What will you say?

When God asks....

*Do you value your friends
as much as they deserve?*

What will you say?

When God asks....

*How long will you leave it
until you live life to the full?*

What will you say?

When God asks....

*Do you pray as much
to thank as to receive?*

What will you say?

When God asks....

What stops you being more optimistic?

What will you say?

When God asks....

Is your appreciation too late, too often?

What will you say?

When God asks....

*How worrying is a problem
when you're not thinking about it?*

What will you say?

When God asks....

*Do you pursue things
you know will hurt you?*

What will you say?

When God asks....

*Does your generosity
match your desire for gain?*

What will you say?

When God asks....

Does feeling guilty help you?

What will you say?

When God asks....

Do you understand that surrender
is letting go, not giving in?

What will you say?

When God asks....

*Why do you miss so much
that is beautiful?*

What will you say?

When God asks....

When will you be satisfied?

What will you say?

When God asks....

*Does your compassion
move you enough to take action?*

What will you say?

When God asks....

*Does your tolerance equal the tolerance
you expect from others?*

What will you say?

When God asks....

Do you refuse to listen to gossip?

What will you say?

When God asks....

*Do you create opportunity
or wait for it?*

What will you say?

When God asks....

Do you give up easily?

What will you say?

When God asks....

Does any possession love you back?

What will you say?

When God asks....

What do you think impresses me?

What will you say?

When God asks....

Which controls your life most,
love or fear?

What will you say?

When God asks....

Are you fun to be with?

What will you say?

When God asks....

*Do you appreciate the living
as much as you grieve the dead?*

What will you say?

When God asks....

Do you ever doubt my ability?

What will you say?

When God asks....

*Do you blame your circumstances
or change them?*

What will you say?

When God asks....

*Do you do things
you know you will regret later?*

What will you say?

When God asks....

Do you make your love conditional?

What will you say?

When God asks....

Do you dare to leap
or do you need to be pushed?

What will you say?

When God asks....

Do you believe in miracles?

What will you say?

When God asks....

*Do you acknowledge your achievements
with the same ease
you acknowledge your failures?*

What will you say?

When God asks....

*Do your fears
live up to your expectations?*

What will you say?

When God asks....

Do you help keep your planet healthy?

What will you say?

When God asks....

Do you sing your own song?

What will you say?

When God asks....

Does your faith allow you to accept
what you don't always understand?

What will you say?

When God asks....

Do you walk in the shadow of others
or do you let your own light shine?

What will you say?

When God asks....

Do you resist change?

What will you say?

When God asks....

*Does someone have to fall
before you help them?*

What will you say?

When God asks....

*Do you limit your dreams
by making them conditional
on becoming realities?*

What will you say?

When God asks....

*Would the world be a better place
if everyone in it
followed your example?*

What will you say?

When God asks....

Do you leave your life to chance
by believing in luck?

What will you say?

When God asks....

Do you give your life purpose?

What will you say?

When God asks....

Do you wish you laughed more?

What will you say?

When God asks....

Could you give more to charity?

What will you say?

When God asks....

Do you wish you took more risks?

What will you say?

When God asks....

Do you think things go wrong
just because they don't turn out
how you would like?

What will you say?

When God asks....

*Do you judge people
by their appearance?*

What will you say?

When God asks....

*Do you know anyone who
has found contentment in money?*

What will you say?

When God asks....

*Does the word 'change' mean
fear or excitement for you?*

What will you say?

When God asks....

Do you need a reason to be happy?

What will you say?

When God asks....

*Do you use the past
as a library or a home?*

What will you say?

When God asks....

Which do you find easier,
trusting or doubting?

What will you say?

When God asks....

*Would you like to have
better thoughts?*

What will you say?

When God asks....

Who controls your thoughts?

What will you say?

When God asks....

*Do you realise
that you can only keep hatred alive
in a memory?*

What will you say?

When God asks....

*Do you use the power of thought
to improve your health?*

What will you say?

When God asks....

*Do you wait for love to come
and knock on your door,
or do you go out and find it
in everything you can?*

What will you say?

When God asks....

*Do you use compromise
to help the pieces fit,
or do you just keep
changing the pieces?*

What will you say?

When God asks....

*Do you like yourself as much
as you want others to like you?*

What will you say?

When God asks....

*Do your mistakes
become lessons or guilt?*

What will you say?

When God asks....

Do you see challenge as struggle?

What will you say?

When God asks....

*Do you put enjoyment into things
or expect to get it out of them?*

What will you say?

When God asks....

*Have you noticed how the priorities
of dying people change?*

What will you say?

When God asks....

Do you see your life as an adventure?

What will you say?

When God asks....

Which is more important to you;
making a living or making a difference?

What will you say?

When God asks....

*Have you found security within yourself
or are you still searching elsewhere?*

What will you say?

When God asks....

How often do you sing out loud?

What will you say?

When God asks....

*Will you die
without really living?*

What will you say?

When God asks....

*Which is your
greatest motivation for change;
pain or pleasure?*

What will you say?

When God asks....

*Are you able to see a competitor
as a potential ally?*

What will you say?

When God asks....

*Do you fear the darkness
or use it as an opportunity to glow?*

What will you say?

When God asks....

Do you learn from children?

What will you say?

When God asks....

Are you ever without hope?

What will you say?

When God asks....

Is your kindness obvious?

What will you say?

When God asks....

Who would impress you most;
Someone who had achieved
real contentment
or someone who had great wealth?

What will you say?

When God asks....

*Do you allow your head
to deprive your heart?*

What will you say?

When God asks....

Do you need to touch to feel?

What will you say?

When God asks....

Can you see order in chaos?

What will you say?

When God asks....

*Could you be more passionate
about your life?*

What will you say?

When God asks....

Do you log the special moments?

What will you say?

When God asks....

Who creates your image,
you or the opinions of others?

What will you say?

When God asks....

*Do you act on the priorities
you voice?*

What will you say?

When God asks....

Do you see children as your equal?

What will you say?

When God asks....

*Do you respect
those who have less than you?*

What will you say?

When God asks....

*Do you extend your kindness
to the unkind?*

What will you say?

When God asks....

*Have you discovered that appreciation
is the brightness control on your life?*

What will you say?

When God asks....

Do you greet the day with gratitude?

What will you say?

When God asks....

How often
are you silent enough to hear me?

What will you say?

When God asks....

*Do you realise only you
can label someone your enemy?*

What will you say?

When God asks....

*Do you use your imagination
to inspire your life?*

What will you say?

When God asks....

*Have you retained the ability
to see with wonderment?*

What will you say?

When God asks....

Can you see courage in humility?

What will you say?

When God asks....

*What question
would you like to ask me?*

What will you say?

When God asks....

*Do you accept
what you cannot change?*

What will you say?

When God asks....

Do you class yourself a failure
even when you have given your best?

What will you say?

When God asks....

Do you accept age with grace?

What will you say?

When God asks....

*Have you made a list of the things
you don't want and haven't got,
to discover how much you really have?*

What will you say?

When God asks....

*Do you greet ignorance with the
understanding it deserves?*

What will you say?

When God asks....

Do you lend what you could give?

What will you say?

When God asks....

Do you judge before you understand?

What will you say?

When God asks....

When you make a mistake,
which helps the most,
understanding or punishment?

What will you say?

When God asks....

Do you receive many thank you cards?

What will you say?

When God asks....

*Have your answers to these questions
shown you that you could
be living a better life?*

What will you say?

When God asks....

Do you know how much I love you?

What will you say?

Special thanks to the following
for believing in & sponsoring
the first printing of this book.

I hope when God asks them
what they did to help others,
they will remember to say:
"I helped make *When God asks*
available to the world".

Mark & Eileen Carr
Carol Abbott
Charles & Laurice Barnescone
Julian Baker & Louise Atwill
Tony & Gill Wilson

Crystal Clear

Crystal Clear
Products to inspire, relax and uplift
01604 604 499

European College of Bowen Studies
The Bowen Technique
Taking light touch therapy to new ground
01373 461 873

Infinite Possibilities Ltd
Achieve amazing results through transformational training
01604 784 331

Motivation & Personal Development
Learning and living with passion
01429 278 854

What's been said (and by who) about Richard and his books

Stella McCartney	'…the books brighten up my day…'
Geri Halliwell	'…these books have inspirational quotations which sort of bully you into feeling better…'
Anthea Turner	'…your books are truly inspirational, especially on the down days we all have, I've read every page.'
Richard Branson	'…how delightful…'
Daily Mail	'…thoughts which make you think about what's important in life…'
Dr Bernie Seigel	'…I heartily endorse your book, I know the wisdom of pain and passion, and you have found it…'
Robert Holden	'…This little book of gems can add sparkle to your life. Read and look carefully…'

New Woman	*'...a must for a stressed out soul...'*
British Reflexology Association	*'...these pocket sized books are filled with a wealth of advice..'*
British Telecom	*'...nothing but praise for the pertinence of the book's contents...'*
Here's Health	*'...profound quotations to lift the spirits...'*
Looking Good	*'...he draws from experiences which sound incredibly far fetched, but really happened to him..'*
Success Now	*'...if ever you needed evidence that success - real success is not just about making money, then this story will convince you...'*
Dr CRM Wilson Consultant Psychiatrist	*'...gems which anybody would find reassuring... a positive attitude to life...'*

About the Author

Richard had never prayed so hard.
The recession had struck, virtually overnight he crashed from
being a self made multi-millionaire to being broke,
alone and terrified on Rock Bottom.

His prayers were answered,
but not in the way he thought.
His mansion, company and bank balance were not returned.
Instead he was shown the true meaning of wealth.

Now he is sharing his message with millions through his
books, seminars and TV appearances.

OTHER PUBLICATIONS BY RICHARD:

150 Ways to make your life Ten out of Ten
ISBN 0 9528198 05

10/10 The Yellow Book
ISBN 0 9528198 13

Mental Tonic
ISBN 0 9528198 80

Collection Box
(all three of the above in a presentation case)
ISBN 0 9528198 48

From Black & White to colour
ISBN 0 9528198 3X

Inner Nutshell Cards
ISBN 0 9528198 21

To be placed on Richard's mailing list,
for details of his seminars and forthcoming works
or if you are unable to obtain
any of his publications please contact:

Ten out of Ten
PO Box 454
Northampton NN4 0GJ

Tel: 01604 761886